Lovely Mandala

This book belongs to:

____

____

____

Thank you

We extend our heartfelt gratitude for choosing our coloring book as your creative companion. Your artistic endeavors have breathed life into the pages, and we are immensely grateful for your support.

We hope our book brought you solace, relaxation, and a momentary escape into a world of vibrant imagination. If you enjoyed the experience and found our coloring book inspiring, we would be thrilled if you could take a moment to share your thoughts by leaving a review.

Your support means everything to us, and we look forward to embarking on more artistic journeys together.

With heartfelt appreciation,
Lena

Lena Sosica Coloring Books

Coloring Tips

For optimal results, we suggest using colored pencils, crayons and gel pens to bring these pages to life. If markers or paints are your preference, just remember to place a protective sheet behind the page you're working on to prevent any potential bleed-through. Happy coloring!

Test Pages for Your Creative Tools

Inside this book, you'll discover two test pages designed specifically for you to experiment with your coloring tools. These pages provide an opportunity to explore your colors and techniques before diving into the main content. Enjoy this creative warm-up as you embark on your coloring journey!

No AI coloring images

In this enchanting collection, you will find no AI-generated images. Each design has been thoughtfully handcrafted, ensuring that your coloring experience is a genuine reflection of human creativity and imagination.

Legal

First paperback edition December 2023

Cover art by Lena Sosica
Layout by Lena Sosica
Illustrations by Lena Sosica

www.lenasosicacoloringbooks.com

Test Page

Test Page